THE TEACHINGS OF

Mormonism

John H. Gerstner

BAKER BOOK HOUSE
Grand Rapids, Michigan 49516

Copyright © 1960 by Baker Books
a division of Baker Book House Company
0. Box 6287, Grand Rapids, MI 49516-6287

Originally appeared as chapter four and appendix in
The Theology of the Major Sects

ISBN: 0-8010-3719-0

Sixteenth printing, May 2002

Printed in the United States of America

For information about academic books, resources for
Christian leaders, and all new releases available from
Baker Book House, visit our web site:
http://www.bakerbooks.com/

Contents

Introduction 5
1 Description and History of Mormonism 7
2 Doctrines of the Mormons 18
3 Terms Frequently Used by the Mormons 23
4 For Further Reading 26
5 Summary of Traditional Christian Doctrines 28
6 Brief Definitions of the Sects 32

Introduction

The abundance of literature on various "sects" shows that there is great interest in the subject. But what is a *sect?* We must make our definition clear, for there is wide difference of opinion on its meaning.

Evangelicals generally use *sect* when referring to those denominations which do not hold to fundamental biblical principles—especially the deity of Christ and His atonement. This booklet is written from the evangelical perspective.

The Teachings of Mormonism is designed as a ready reference booklet. It is meant to be a quick guide to the wealth of literature on this subject, and it includes a valuable table and glossary.

The general exposition in the first chapter gives an easily-grasped overview of the sect. The following chapter, "Doctrines of Mormonism," provides the reference material which summarizes the first chapter and adds some more technical data. Chapter two contains the basic theological structure of Mormonism, stated objectively and concisely. The text itself gives a fuller exposition of some of the cardinal points outlined in the first chapter.

Chapter three, "Terms Frequently Used by Mormons," gives some of the most common terms in the vocabulary of this sect. Sects often have their own precise definitions for common religious words, and the glossary makes this immediately evident.

Chapter four, "For Further Reading," lists both primary and secondary sources for further study of the theology and practice of the sect.

A summary of the essential teachings of traditional Christianity appears in chapter five. This summary is included to provide a basis for comparison with the doctrines of Mormonism. This chapter is designed to be used as a frame of reference.

To make the theologies of different sects clearer, their teachings have been summarized in the "Chart of Comparative Doctrines" at the end of chapter six. This tabular outline classifies the doctrines of each group in relation to the tenets of orthodox Christianity. Beginning with the doctrines of the Seventh-day Adventists, and continuing with the teachings of the Jehovah's Witnesses, Mormons, and Christian Scientists, this chart allows the reader to see at a glance the position of each group on various Christian doctrines.

1 Description and History of Mormonism

The Mormons were driven from Ohio, Mississippi, and Illinois, and finally found rest in unoccupied Mexican territory. (This later became American land, in spite of the Mormons' vigorous opposition to the "Gentiles.") While Mormonism has never quite come to terms with America, it is still unquestionably the most native of all American religious groups.

> Its Bible came into being at Palmyra, New York, it proclaimed Zion first in Illinois and later in Utah, its prophet's name was Smith, its sacred history deals with North and South America, with landmarks familiar to us all, and not with events in far off Judea. Its exodus took place across the plains of our continent, its Red Sea was the Mississippi, and when the last trump sounds Jesus is coming to American soil, with headquarters in Salt Lake City.[1]

Joseph Smith

It all began in Sharon, Vermont. Today a thirty-eight-and-a-half-foot monument stands to Joseph Smith, who was "martyred" thirty-eight and a half years after being born in this small town. The inscription reads: "Sacred to the memory of Joseph Smith, the Prophet, born here 23rd December, 1805, martyred at Carthage, Illinois, 27th June, 1844." If Sharon today is proud to have cradled the Mormon idol, it was not always so, judging from an old New England gazetteer which confessed: " 'This is the birthplace of that infamous impostor, the Mormon prophet Joseph Smith, a dubious honor Sharon would relinquish willingly to another town.' "[2]

Joseph Smith can not be called a "root out of a dry ground." His resemblance to his father brings to mind the remark William Pitt (the younger) made in his maiden speech in Parliament: "This is not a chip off the old block; it is the old block himself." Joseph Smith, Sr. was a prophet in his own right—as his son seems to have appreciated, judging from the striking similarity between two of their alleged visions. And Lucy Mack Smith likewise was a worthy mother of the prophet, for she was the daughter of Solomon Mack, who displayed some knack for the occult. She was what we would today call "psychic," judging from her reputation among some neighbors. With such parents it is not surprising that Smith's youth could be summed up by his principal biographer as that of "a likable ne'er-do-well who was notorious for

---

[1] Charles W. Ferguson, *The Confusion of Tongues*, p. 366.
[2] Fawn M. Brodie, *No Man Knows My History. The Life of Joseph Smith the Mormon Prophet*, p. 1.

tall tales and necromantic arts and who spent his leisure leading a band of idlers in digging for buried treasure."[3] He had a highly imaginative disposition of his own, which was fanned by religious fanaticism rampant around Palmyra, New York (where his family now lived). With such a background it was not surprising that Joseph Smith would, in 1820, have his first vision.

Three more years passed, however, before there came the dream to end all dreams. Not far from Palmyra, according to Smith, appeared a resurrected saint, the angel Moroni, who had died about A.D. 400. He gave Joseph Smith an important message. It seems that Moroni had been the son of Mormon and the last of the Nephites, which were crushed out by the rival Lamanites. The whole story was recorded on certain golden plates which Moroni had hidden under the hill Cumorah until the appointed time for their disclosure to the prophet of the Latter-day Church. Joseph greatly desired the valuable plates, but was rebuked and told he could not have them for four more years. During the interval he was to revisit Cumorah every year.

In 1827 Smith was permitted to take the plates home, and another three years passed before these, inscribed in "Reformed Egyptian hieroglyphics," were translated by Smith (using his personal Rosetta stone, called the Urim and Thummim). Behind a sheet which was suspended by a rope, he looked into his peepstone and translated the inspired words to his secretary, Martin Harris, who was on the other side of the curtain. Harris' profane eyes were forbidden to behold the celestial plates on pain of immediate death at the hands of the enraged deity. Oliver Cowdery, being more literate, later replaced Harris. Finally in 1830, the new revelation was published at Palmyra, and the existence of the plates certified by the three witnesses who, probably under the influence of the prophet, saw them with the "eyes of faith."

In August, the Church of Christ (later, of the Latter-day Saints) was formed by six people meeting at Fayette, New York. The first 100 percent American church was born.

From this time on, the prophet was largely without honor in his own country. In 1831, he found it advisable to leave New York for Kirtland, Ohio. From here, because of various offenses culminating in a huge bank fraud, he and the saints found it expedient to move to the American Zion in Missouri. There the Gentiles fought him, imprisoned him, and finally drove him out to take his refuge in a city of his own making on the banks of the Mississippi, Nauvoo, Illinois. From this place he was driven off the planet altogether, killed by some lawless militia at a nearby prison in 1844.

---

[3]Ibid., p. 16.

Brigham Young

In 1847 Brigham Young, substituting hard-headed business effi-
ciency for revelations and visions, removed the harassed saints out of
civilized America to distant Utah. There they were destined to make
the desert blossom as the rose and again become a part of the United
States, from which they thought they had fled. Now a million strong
and reconciled to the Gentiles (and the Gentiles to them), both are
living together more or less happily.

The Theology of Mormonism

What beliefs motivated the Mormon movement and helped make it
what it has become? Fortunately, for our purposes, there is a brief,
innocuous summary of Mormon doctrine by the prophet himself.
Joseph Smith received the revelation of the "Articles of Faith of the
Church of Jesus Christ of Latter-Day Saints." It consists of thirteen
brief general statements on the main points of Mormon belief. Although it is in itself not very instructive, when the outline is filled out
with other statements of Smith and other authorities it can provide a
fairly clear understanding of the theology of the Latter-day Saints.

Article 1. "We believe in God, the Eternal Father, and in His Son,
Jesus Christ, and in the Holy Ghost."

> The Mormon doctrine of God embraces the following points: (a) There are
> many gods: 'Are there more Gods than one? Yes, many' (Cat., 13). (b) These
> gods are polygamous or 'sealed' human beings grown divine: 'God himself was
> once as we now are, and is an exalted Man' (Brigham Young, J. of D., VI:4);
> 'And you have got to learn how to be Gods yourself, the same as all Gods have
> done before you' (Ibid.); 'Then shall they [that have been 'sealed' in marriage]
> be Gods, because they have all power, and the angels are subject unto them'
> (D. and C., 467). (c) Adam is the God of this world: 'He [Adam] is our Father
> and our God, and the only God with whom we have to do' (Brigham Young, J.
> of D., I:50). (d) These Gods have fleshly bodies: 'There is no other God in
> heaven but that God who has flesh and bones' (Smith, Comp., 287). (e) They
> are polygamous: 'When our Father Adam came into the garden of Eden, he
> came with a celestial body, and brought Eve, one of his wives, with him'
> (Young, J. of D., I:50). (f) They have children forever: 'Each God, through his
> wife, or wives, raises up a numerous family of sons and daughters: . . . for each
> father and mother will be in a condition to multiply forever and ever' (The
> Seer, I:37).[4]

D. M. McAllister also makes perfectly clear that God is a literal
Father:

> Neither can that most filial word, Father, as so often lovingly uttered by our
> Elder Brother (Christ), be regarded as a merely figurative expression; it was
> always clearly evident that he meant it for an actual, not figurative, declara-

---

[4]James Henry Snowden, *The Truth about Mormonism*, N. Y., 1926, pp. 128f. Cf. also
Pratt, *Key to the Science of Theology*, p. 42.

tion. He was in very deed a Son of the Most High, in his spirit, just as he was also a Son when his spirit body was combined with his earthly tabernacle, when born of his divinely selected mother in the flesh.[5]

It is already manifest that Joseph Smith's confession, "We believe in God, the Eternal Father" is a horrid travesty of what those words usually signify in the creeds of Christendom.[6]

The following phrase, "and in His Son, Jesus Christ," is just as misleading. Jesus pre-existed. But this is true of all human beings: they pre-exist as the spirit children of the Gods, waiting for incarnate men to provide them bodies by procreation. These bodies they then inhabit.[7] So pre-existence itself is nothing unique. Jesus was, however, in His preincarnate state, Jehovah, the agent of the Father God, Elohim. But Christ was unique in His birth, for the Mormons have a doctrine of the virgin birth. Brigham Young states: "When the Virgin Mary conceived the child Jesus, the father had begotten him in his own likeness. He was NOT begotten by the Holy Ghost. And who was the Father? He was the first of the human family. . . . Jesus, our elder brother, was begotten in the flesh by the same character that was in the garden of Eden, and who is our Father in Heaven."[8]

Mormonism also has a doctrine of the exaltation of Jesus Christ. He is exalted to become equal with God the Father, another travesty of the Biblical doctrine, which maintains that He always was an equal member of the Godhead and that His exaltation consisted only in the elevation of His humanity (His deity was incapable of further elevation). McAllister is aglow with the thrill of this "exaltation" of Christ, which is really a base humiliation. "What! Our Elder Brother, Jesus Christ, to be 'equal with God,' the Father! Yes, that was his glorious destiny; he is one with God the Father!" Having thus humiliated Christ far below what He actually is, McAllister then elevates man, saying, "and 'we are heirs of God, and joint heirs with Christ' (Romans 8:17), if we follow in his footsteps."[9]

The Holy Ghost is the only traditional member of the Godhead who in Mormonism retains His spirituality or rather, refined materiality. For, as Joseph Smith said, " 'There is no such thing as immaterial matter. All spirit is matter, but is more fine or pure, and can only be discerned by purer eyes.' "[10]

Article 2. "We believe that men will be punished for their own sins, and not for Adam's transgression."

[5]McAllister, *Life's Greatest Questions — What Am I?*, p. 5.
[6]Cf. B. H. Roberts, *The Lord Hath Spoken*, pp. 3f.
[7]James E. Talmage, *Articles of Faith*, 12th ed., Salt Lake City, 1924, pp. 465ff.
[8]Young, *Journal of Discourses*, I:50.
[9]*Life's Greatest Questions*, p. 11.
[10]*Compendium of Mormon Doctrine*, p. 259, cited in Snowden, *Truth about Mormonism*, p. 130.

Denying the responsibility of men for the sin of their great representative Adam, in whom the Bible says all sinned, by implication does away with original sin. The Mormons also deny the inherited contamination of children: "Wherefore little children are whole, for they are not capable of committing sin; wherefore the curse of Adam is taken from them in me [Christ], that it hath no power over them; and the law of circumcision is done away in me. . . . And their little children need no repentance, neither baptism. . . . Behold, I say unto you, that he that supposeth little children need baptism, is in the gall of bitterness, and in the bonds of iniquity; . . . wherefore should he be cut off while in the thought, he must go down to hell."[11]

Not only do the Mormons believe that other persons cannot be responsible for Adam's sin. Strictly speaking, they hold that even Adam cannot be, for his sin was not a sin and his fall was a fall upward. Mormonism clearly makes Adam's "sin" a necessary and inevitable thing that effected a great advantage for mankind. Thus Talmage states:

> Adam found himself in a position that impelled him to disobey one of the requirements of God. He and his wife had been commanded to multiply and replenish the earth. Adam was still immortal; Eve had come under the penalty of mortality; and in such dissimilar conditions the two could not remain together, and therefore could not fulfil the divine requirement. On the other hand, Adam would be disobeying another command by yielding to his wife's request. He deliberately and wisely decided to stand by the first and greater commandment; and, therefore, with a full comprehension of the nature of his act, he also partook of the fruit that grew on the tree of knowledge. The fact that Adam acted understandingly in this matter is affirmed by the scriptures. . . .[12]

The Mormon Catechism puts the whole matter more briefly and bluntly:

"Was it necessary that Adam should partake of the forbidden fruit? Answer: Yes, unless he had done so he would not have known good and evil here, neither could he have had moral posterity. . . . Did Adam and Eve lament or rejoice because they had transgressed the commandment? Answer: They rejoiced and praised God."

Elder McAllister also makes necessity out of free choice and a virtue out of necessity. "The earthly bodies of Adam and Eve," he writes, "were, no doubt, intended by the Heavenly Father to be immortal tabernacles for their spirits, but it was necessary for them to pass through mortality and be redeemed through the sacrifice made by Jesus Christ that the fulness of life might come. Therefore they disobeyed God's command. . . ."[13]

---

[11]*Book of Mormon; Doctrine and Covenants*, pp. 18f., cited in Van Baalen, *The Chaos of Cults*, 1956 edition, p. 179.

[12]Talmage, *Articles of Faith*, p. 68.

[13]*Life's Greatest Questions*, p. 11.

This type of thinking makes God appear foolish, since it seems that the only way man can carry out God's purpose is to disobey His commandments; or, to carry out one commandment he must disobey another. In order to preserve God's best interests, man must devise his own best strategy; very much the way a wise and experienced elder counselor of state would advise a young and inexperienced monarch. To make the matter worse, the real thinker and wise counselor in this whole affair is the devil himself. So, instead of tempting Adam and Eve to evil, he was giving counsel of perfection; and instead of frustrating God, he was advising what was necessary for God to accomplish His purposes. One is reminded of the Ophites, or serpent worshipers, in the ancient church, who consistently adored the serpent because his temptation was regarded as an invitation to progress.

Article 3. "We believe that through the Atonement of Christ, all mankind may be saved, by obedience to the laws and ordinances of the Gospel."

What kind of atonement can there be in a system in which sin is a work of necessity and virtue? Atonement has a place, but an utterly adventitious one. John Taylor states: " 'In the first place, according to justice, men could not have been redeemed from temporal death, except through the atonement of Jesus Christ; and in the second place, they could not be redeemed from spiritual death, only through obedience to His law. . . .' "[14] This statement, like Smith's, is mere statement without explanation. One looks in vain for a real conception of atonement or expiation in the Morman scheme of salvation. The word is used without any concrete meaning, and one wonders if the word is used because of traditional Christianity rather than because of any inherent place in this system.

The companion statement ("may be saved, by obedience to the laws and ordinances of the Gospel"), following a reference to an atonement which lacks real meaning, surely suggests a legalistic doctrine of salvation. Furthermore, the explicit rejection of justification by faith, which is said to have "exercised an influence for evil since the early days of Christianity," confirms this deduction.[15]

It is at this point that polygamy comes into the Mormon system. (Polygamy is clearly a part of the Mormon scheme of salvation.) Here are what seem to be the steps by which the Latter-day Saints arrive at their belief in polygamy:

(1) The Gods have begotten a host of spirit children.

(2) These are restless spirits until they are clothed with a body.

---

[14]*The Mediation and Atonement,* p. 170, cited by Van Baalen, *Chaos of Cults,* 2nd revised and enlarged edition, 1956, p. 180.

[15]Talmage, *Articles of Faith,* p. 120.

(3) Bodies for the spirit-children are provided by human procreation. Therefore, man's chief end is to glorify the Gods and have
babies.

(4) Hence, procreation becomes man's primary duty.

(5) The more children a person has, the more virtuous he is.

This line of reasoning would appear to lead to polygamy. But
monogamy was so clearly taught in the Bible, especially in the words
of Christ, and so universally accepted by the Christian churches, that
early Mormonism in the *Book of Mormon* advocated it.

Joseph Smith's actual practice preceded his pretended revelation on
the subject setting aside the teaching of the Bible and the *Book of
Mormon*. His pretended "Revelation on the Eternity of the Marriage
Covenant, including Plurality of Wives, Given through Joseph, the
Seer, in Nauvoo, Hancock County, Illinois, July 12th, 1843" is as
follows:

> And again as pertaining to the law of the Priesthood: If any man espouse a
> virgin, and desire to espouse another, and the first give her consent; and if he
> espouse the second, and they are virgins, and have vowed to no other man,
> then he is justified; he cannot commit adultery, for they are given unto him;
> for he cannot commit adultery with that that belongeth to him and no one
> else. And if he have ten virgins given unto him by this law, he cannot commit
> adultery for they belong to him, and they are given unto him, therefore he is
> justified.

Polygamy would presumably not require any other inducements to
make it agreeable to certain men; but the women would not,
naturally, find it so attractive. Hence the Mormons developed a doctrine that a woman cannot be saved without being "sealed" to a man.
Sealing may be effected without actual cohabitation; this has frequently been done, even in the case of the prophet himself.

Polygamy has now been categorically repudiated by Utah officials
and probably is very rarely practiced, though twenty fundamentalists
went to prison for it in 1946. The principle remains a blemish on the
religion of Joseph Smith. An unfortunate footnote to all this is the
oft-quoted remark of Brigham Young: "Jesus Christ was a polygamist;
Mary and Martha, the sisters of Lazarus, were his plural wives, and
Mary Magdalene was another. Also, the bridal feast of Cana of Galilee,
where Jesus turned the water into wine, was on the occasion of one of
his own marriages."[16]

Article 4. "We believe that the first principles and ordinances of the
Gospel are: (1) Faith in the Lord Jesus Christ; (2) Repentance;
(3) Baptism by immersion for the remission of sins; (4) Laying on of
hands for the gift of the Holy Ghost."

---

[16]*Journal of Discourses*, I:50.

Article 5. "We believe that a man must be called of God, by prophecy, and by the laying on of hands, by those who are in authority to preach the Gospel and administer in the ordinances thereof."

Article 6. "We believe in the same organization that existed in the Primitive Church, viz., apostles, prophets, pastors, teachers, evangelists, etc."

In these sections we find the doctrine of a group that considers itself the exclusively true church. All other denominations are outside the pale. This notion harks back to Smith's first revelation, which he was hoping would show him which denomination to join. It instead showed him the way out of them all. From then on it became a duty for all followers of the prophet to follow him out of their churches. Later Smith said, "Any person who shall be so wicked as to receive a holy ordinance of the gospel from the ministers of these apostate churches will be sent down to hell with them, unless he repents of the unholy and impious act."[17] The *Elders' Journal* took up the same refrain: "We shall see all the priests who adhere to the sectarian religions of the day, with all their followers without one exception, receive their portion with the Devil and his angels."[18] Frightening the sheep out of other folds, Mormonism corralled them in its own by the famous gathering act of 1830.

Church Organization

The actual organization of the Church of the Latter-day Saints is almost as complicated, efficient, and autocratic as the Roman Catholic Church. The autocratic character of the Mormon system is well stated by Fawn Brodie:

> Basically, therefore, the church organization remained autocratic; only the trappings were democratic. The membership voted on the church officers twice a year. But there was only one slate of candidates, and it was selected by the first presidency, comprised of Joseph himself and his two counselors. Approval or disapproval was indicated by a standing vote in the general conference. Dissenting votes became so rare that the elections came to be called—and the irony was unconscious—the 'sustaining of the authorities.'[19]

This was in Joseph Smith's day; Brigham Young was more autocratic still. It is doubtful that the basic character of the hierarchy has changed much today.

Probably the most novel of the Mormon rites is that of baptism for the dead. This is an instance of extreme literalism. Mistaking Paul's mysterious words in I Corinthians 15:29, Mormons baptize the dead,

---

[17]*The Seer*, Vols. I and II, p. 255, cited by Snowden, *Truth about Mormonism*, p. 134.
[18]August, 1838, pp. 59f., cited in La Rue, p. 45.
[19]Brodie, *No Man Knows*, p. 162.

believing that they cannot be saved without the rite. Penrose tells how Mormons feel on the subject:

> Millions of earth's sons and daughters have passed out of the body without obeying the law of baptism. Many of them will gladly accept the word and law of the Lord when it is proclaimed to them in the spirit world. But they cannot there attend to ordinances that belong to the sphere which they have left. Can nothing be done in their case? Must they forever be shut out of the kingdom of heaven? Both justice and mercy join in answering 'yes' to the first and 'no' to the last question. What, then, is the way of their deliverance? The living may be baptized for the dead. Other essential ordinances may be attended to vicariously. This glorious truth, hidden from human knowledge for centuries, has been made known in this greatest of all divine dispensations. . . . It gives men and women the power to become 'Saviours on Mount Zion,' Jesus being the great Captain in the army of redeemers.[20]

Marcus Bach in his *Faith and My Friends* tells of an interesting encounter with a Mormon to whom he put the question, "How far does the church intend to go in this ritual? Does it expect to baptize someone for each of the early Americans and the early Protestants and even farther back than that?" To which he received this answer from his Mormon missionary friend: "As far back as Adam! That is part of the great Mormon commission. I intend to have baptism made for my ancestors as far back as I can. So does every active Mormon. The church has the most complete genealogical system in the world. It has on file nearly ten million names already. Missionaries work on these genealogies wherever they go. Everyone helps. Everyone should help to bring together into one family all who have ever lived, and all who are yet to be born for the number of those who are to be born is predetermined. Their souls already exist in the realms of God. Isn't it a wonderful thought? We come from God and we return to God to be like Him. I expect someday to sit down with those I have known in a pre-existence and in this existence. I expect to talk with Joseph Smith and Brigham Young and all the other prophets. And I fully expect to talk with God."[21]

Article 7. "We believe in the gift of tongues, prophecy, revelation, visions, healing, interpretation of tongues, etc."

Article 8. "We believe the Bible to be the word of God as far as it is translated correctly; we also believe the Book of Mormon to be the word of God."

Article 9. "We believe all that God has revealed, all that He does now reveal, and we believe that He will yet reveal many great and important things pertaining to the Kingdom of God."

---

[20]Penrose, *Mormon Doctrine*, p. 48, cited by Van Baalen, *Chaos of Cults*, 1956 edition, p. 180.
[21]*Faith and My Friends*, p. 277.

Article 10. "We believe in the literal gathering of Israel and in the restoration of the Ten Tribes; that Zion will be built upon this [the American] continent; that Christ will reign personally upon the earth; and, that the earth will be renewed and receive its paradisiacal glory."

This is a fairly conventional sort of millennialism—except for the American locale. But this article gives us very little of the full eschatology of the Mormons. For one thing, Mormons believe that the righteous go immediately to be in paradise and await the resurrection. After the resurrection, it appears that there will be the final disposition of all men. Some go to hell. Joseph Smith said that the number who went to hell could be counted on the fingers of one hand. From this remark it can be concluded that Mormonism is a form of Universalism. It is difficult to reconcile this report, however, with the afore-quoted remark of Smith that all who impenitently receive rites from Christian clergymen will perish in hell.

There are three grades in the Mormon heaven: celestial, terrestrial, and telestial. The last, being of inferior glory, seems to be located on other planets; the first is the full heaven reserved for those who have died in the Mormon faith. There are apparently two kinds of beings in heaven. One is the angel, or resurrected being; the other is the unembodied spirit of the just men made perfect.[22]

Article 11. "We claim the privilege of worshiping Almighty God according to the dictates of our own conscience, and allow all men the same privilege, let them worship how, where, or what they may."

This sounds quite American, but as James Snowden says, it is not easy to reconcile such statements with the following from the prophet: "I say, rather than apostates should flourish here, I will unsheath my bowie knife, and conquer or die. Now, you nasty apostates, clear out, or judgment will be put to the line.... I want you to hear, bishops, what I am about to tell you: Kick these men out of your wards."[23]

Article 12. "We believe in being subject to kings, presidents, rulers, and magistrates, in obeying, honoring, and sustaining the law."

This statement would truly reflect Mormon history and principles if these few words were added: "that is, whenever we find it to be consistent with our doctrine or absolutely necessary." Otherwise, it sounds too much like another official deliverance given out to "fool the Gentiles." Utah was finally subjected to the authority of the United States government only after the most determined opposition of the Saints. Then and then only did Utah become obedient to the laws of the land. Only when the very property of the whole Mormon

---

[22]Cf. Joseph Smith, *Doctrine and Covenants,* p. 132.
[23]*Journal of Discourses,* I:80, cited by Snowden, *Truth about Mormonism,* p. 134.

church was threatened by the government did Mormonism yield to the authority of government and officially forbid polygamy. It is all right to let bygones be bygones and forget the past if Mormonism is as patriotic and loyal as it appears today. But we must not forget the principles that are still on the books, such as this statement of Apostle John Taylor:

> The priesthood holds "the power and right to give laws and commandments to individuals, churches, rulers, nations and the world; to appoint, ordain and establish constitutions and kingdoms; to appoint kings, presidents, governors, or judges" (Key, p. 70). The priesthood "is the legitimate rule of God, whether in the heavens or on the earth, and it is the only legitimate power that has a right to rule on the earth; and when the will of God is done on the earth as it is in heaven, no other power will be or rule."[24]

Article 13. "We believe in being honest, true, chaste, benevolent, virtuous, and in doing good to all men; indeed, we may say that we follow the admonition of Paul—We believe all things, we hope all things, we have endured many things, and hope to be able to endure all things. If there is anything virtuous, lovely, or of good report or praiseworthy, we seek after these things."

We do not intend to probe the motives of the Mormons nor do we find any relish in questioning their good intentions, nor in denying their achievement of certain worthy goals. But insofar as they have anything of which to be proud, it may be traced to their residuum of Bible faith.

---

[24]Snowden, ibid., p. 138.

2 Doctrines of the Mormons

Doctrine of the Bible

"We believe the Bible to be the word of God, as far as it is translated correctly; we also believe the Book of Mormon to be the word of God" (Joseph Smith, *Articles of Faith,* Article 8). In addition to these books, the church adopted Joseph Smith's *Doctrine and Covenants* and *The Pearl of Great Price* as authoritative (Talmage, *Articles of Faith,* p. 5), but the Bible and Book of Mormon are far more influential. Furthermore, "The Book of Mormon 'in no sense supplants the Bible, but supports it' " (Paul Hanson, *Jesus Christ among Ancient Americans,* p. 143; cited by Braden, *These Also Believe,* p. 438; cf. Talmage, *AF,* p. 236). "About one-eighteenth of the book [of Mormon] is taken from the Bible, no credit being given for this in the earliest editions, but in the present edition proper credit is given. The following chapters are taken bodily: Isa. 2 to 14, 18, 19, 21, 48, 49, 50, 51, 52, 54; Matt. 5, 6, 7; I Cor. 13. Besides these chapters, from page 2 to page 428 contain 298 direct quotations from the New Testament . . ." (Snowden, *Truth about Mormonism,* p. 101). Concerning the Book of Mormon, "more has been written about [its] divine authenticity . . . than about any other moot matter on the human record, unless it be the Genesis account of creation" (Ferguson, *The Confusion of Tongues,* p. 368). Joseph Smith claimed to find plates written by the angel Moroni which he translated as the Book of Mormon. Most non-Mormon students are convinced that the Book of Mormon was actually drawn from the unpublished *Manuscript Found* (not *Manuscript Story*) by Spaulding (Brodie, *NMK,* Appendix B). Constant revisions have been made—more than three thousand changes since the first edition. The principal content of the Book of Mormon is the narrative of the dispersal of the Jews, after their captivity, and their settlement and struggle in America.

Doctrine of God

"We believe in God, the Eternal Father, and in His Son, Jesus Christ, and in the Holy Ghost" (Smith, *AF,* Article I; cf. Cowles, "Church of Jesus Christ of Latter-Day Saints" in Ferm [ed.], *Religion in the Twentieth Century,* p. 288). This is not a Trinity of three persons in one God, for the Mormon Catechism teaches many gods (answer to question 13). These many gods are human beings grown divine: "God himself was once as we now are, and is an exalted man"

(Brigham Young, *Journal of Discourses,* VI, p. 4). "The Father has a body of flesh and bones as tangible as man's" (Joseph Smith, *Doctrine and Covenants,* CXXX, 22; CXXXI, 7). This is the teaching of Joseph Smith, Brigham Young, Orson Pratt, Parley Pratt, James E. Talmage. Roberts argues from the physicality of the son, Christ, that the Father must also be physical (*The Lord Hath Spoken,* p. 314). The Gods not only have bodies and wives, but are polygamous, with an endless progeny of children. A favorite Mormon hymn contains this prayer: "When I leave this frail existence, When I lay this mortal by, Father, Mother, may I meet You, In your royal courts on high."

The only difference between the Holy Spirit and the other gods is that the Holy Spirit has a more refined materiality (Smith, *Compendium of Doctrine,* p. 259). All spirit is material, and all matter is eternal. God "certainly did not create in the sense of bringing into primal existence the ultimate elements of the materials of which the earth consists, for the 'elements are eternal' " (Talmage, *AF,* p. 466, cited by Braden, *TAB,* p. 441; cf. Smith, *DC,* XCIII: 33).

Doctrine of Man

"As man is, God once was; as God is, men may be" (Talmage). All Gods were originally men, and all men are destined to become Gods. Therefore, Brigham Young could say, "You have got to learn to be gods yourselves, and to be kings and priests to God, the same as all gods have done before you" (*JD,* VI, 4). That quotation seems to suggest a God above the gods, but there appears to be nothing but a difference of degree between God and gods. Mormonism appears to be henotheistic, having one god supreme in a pantheon. Men, who are destined to become gods, were pre-existent. Only their present bodily organization is acquired by being born into this world. Morgan argues that God promised eternal life "before the world began" (Titus 1:2); so Paul must have been there to hear this promise made before the world began (*The Plan of Salvation,* p. 6). "We were numbered among 'the sons of God [who] shouted for joy' when the foundation of this earth was laid (Job 38:4-7) and we saw the rebellious Lucifer and his followers cast out of heaven" (McAllister, *Life's Greatest Questions,* p. 9). The Mormons show concern for the body's welfare by their strict dietary and health laws, but more than this "the Mormons exalt intelligence and learning."

Doctrine of Sin

As observed above, the gods are constantly begetting children, but these are "spirit" children, without bodies. It is not quite clear how the first humans to live on this earth, Adam and Eve, received bodies, but somehow they did and began the process of human procreation— whereby bodies are produced for the spirit children. But at the very beginning of the process of human generation, sin entered (necessarily). "The earthly bodies of Adam and Eve, no doubt, were intended by the Heavenly Father to be immortal tabernacles for their spirits, but it was necessary for them to pass through mortality and be redeemed through the sacrifice made by Jesus Christ that the fulness of life might come. Therefore they disobeyed God's commands . . ." (McAllister, *LGQ*, p. 11). Thus the fall of man was necessary—it became necessary for men to disobey God in order to do His will (Talmage, *Articles of Faith*, p. 68; *Book of Mormon*, 2 Nephi i. 8).

Concerning the transmission of sin to Adam's posterity, Mormons take a negative position: "We believe that men will be punished for their own sins, and not for Adam's transgression" (Talmage, *AF*, p. 1). Having rejected the doctrine of the imputation of the guilt of sin, Latter-day Saints likewise repudiate the transmission of inherent corruption, or original sin (Joseph Smith, *Doctrine and Covenants*, 18, 19).

Doctrine of Christ

The Christology of the Mormons is rather complicated. (1) Jesus, the pre-existent spirit, is the Son of the Father-God. (2) As such, He is called Jehovah in this prenatal state. (3) As Jehovah, He is the Creator of the world. (4) Being the Creator, He is called the Father. (5) Thus, in a sense, He is the Father and the Son. (6) The birth of Jesus is often spoken of, but the reference apparently applies only to the body which this pre-existent spirit took when He was born in this world. (7) The body of Jesus was the product of the union of the Father-God and the virgin Mary. Brigham Young very plainly teaches that this union between the Father-God and the virgin, which produced the body of Jesus, was physical (8) The pre-existent Jehovah now in the flesh as Jesus Christ becomes "equal with God" and "one with God." (9) Those who follow Jesus will become His heirs and, like Him, equal with and one with God (*Book of Mormon*, Ether 3:14; Young, *Journal of Discourses*, I:50; McAllister, *Life's Greatest Questions*, p. ii; Talmage, AF, pp. 465 f.; Van Baalen, *The Chaos of Cults*, p. 163; Braden, *TAB*, p. 441).

Doctrine of Redemption

It seems that the death of Christ canceled the necessity of man's dying. And with this penalty of sin removed by the atonement, man is apparently then in a position of earn his own salvation by his obedience to the law and gospel (John Taylor, *The Mediation and Atonement*, p. 170, cited by Van Baalen, *CC*, p. 158). That the works of Mormonism are considered meritorious and deserving is clear. Consistently, justification by faith is rejected (Talmage, *AF*, p. 120).

The Mormon record for outwardly good works is contradictory. A reputation for temperance, honesty, patriotic zeal (once they were subjugated), large, stable families, and care for their health is to the credit of the Latter-day Saints. On the other hand, Brigham Young himself accused them of great profanity, and some pirating (*JD*, i, 211, etc.); an eye-witness has described very immoral conditions at times (cited by Stenhouse, *Rocky Mountain Saints*, p. 188), and their official journals showed them against abolition (*Elders' Journal*, July, 1838; *Millennial Star*, vol. 15, pp. 739 ff.; William Earle La Rue, *The Foundations of Mormonism*, p. 27). Their greatest moral defect, however, is polygamy.

Doctrine of the Church

"A revelation in the summer of 1830 was the basis of . . . the 'doctrine of the gathering of the Saints.' The Saints, having been chosen out of the world, were to gather together in one place 'upon the face of this land to prepare their hearts and be prepared in all things against the day when tribulation and desolation are sent forth upon the wicked' " (Braden, *TAB*, pp. 432 f.; cf. *DC*, sect. 29, vss. 7-8). This separation of Mormon from non-Mormon churches is maintained in much literature, as in *The Seer's* statement that apostate churches, if impenitent, will be cast down to hell (II, 255, quoted by Snowden, *The Truth about Mormonism*, p. 134; cf. to same effect, Orson Pratt, Orson Spencer, Brigham Young, Penrose, and others; Van Baalen, *CC*, p. 159; H. Davies, *Christian Deviations*, p. 78; H. C. Sheldon, *A Fourfold Test of Mormonism*, pp. 99 f.). La Rue cites the *Elders' Journal* of 1838, (pp. 59f.), to the same effect.

The Mormons compare with the Jehovah's Witnesses in their high and efficient degree of ecclesiastical organization. The two priesthoods form the basic hierarchical structure. Of these the Melchizedek Priesthood is supreme in spiritual things and consists of the following: (1) The presidency—made up of three men, although the first president really has absolute power; (2) Twelve apostles who appoint the other officials, administer sacraments, and govern between presidents; (3) Patriarch who blesses the members with the blessing of prophecy; (4) High priesthood, which consists of the presidents of the stakes of Zion; (5) The Seventies, or missionaries in groups of seventy; (6) Elders who preach, baptize, and impart the Holy Spirit by imposition of hands.

The second priesthood is the Aaronic, which consists of the following: (1) Presiding bishopric of three bishops in presiding council who collect tithes, care for the poor; (2) Priests who expound the Bible, baptize, administer the Lord's Supper; (3) Teachers who assist the priests and watch that no iniquity occurs; (4) Deacons who assist the teachers and expound the Bible (Julius Bodensieck, *Isms New and Old*, p. 86).

With respect to the state, Smith wrote, "We believe in being subject to kings." On the other hand, some Mormon theologians, such as Apostle John Taylor, taught that the priesthood was superior in authority to the secular power (*Key to Theology*, p. 77; cf. Snowden, *TM*, p. 138). Mormon history seems to suggest that the reconciliation of these two ideas is that authority resides essentially in the hierarchy, but since force is the prerogative of the secular government, subservience is a duty. This interpretation appears evident in the relinquishing of the practice of polygamy because of the law of the land.

Mormonism has some ordinances common to Christendom and some peculiar to itself. Mormons believe in "baptism by immersion for the remission of sins" (*AF*, p. 4). Since none can enter heaven without baptism, Mormons are busily baptizing many dead persons by proxy. Smith also taught in the Articles of Faith the "Laying on of hands for the gift of the Holy Ghost" (*AF*, p. 1, article 4). In addition to the conventional marriage ceremony, the Saints have a unique "sealing" ceremony. A man who died childless may have children raised to him by wives "sealed" to him. In this case, a man on earth is appointed to serve in place of the dead man, in begetting children for him (cf. Blunt, *Dictionary of Sects and Heresies*, p. 352; Louis Binder, *Modern Religious Cults and Society*, p. 151). Another unique rite is the shedding of the blood of certain grievous sinners in a secret way called "blood atonement" (cf. *Journal of Discourses*, iv, 219; William Alexander Linn, *The Story of the Mormons*, pp. 454 f.; Cannon and Knapp, pp. 266 f.; Sheldon, *FTM*, pp. 123 f.; Stenhouse, *RMS*, pp. 292 f.; Hyde, *M*, pp. 179 f.; Snowden, *TM*, p. 132). A woman's hope of salvation is being sealed to a man who will call her forth on the day of resurrection (Smith, *DC*, sect. cxxxii, vss. 15-20; Mayer, *RBA*, p. 454, footnote 30; Braden, *TAB*, p. 446).

Doctrine of the Future

The Mormons teach a rather common variety of the premillennial reign of Christ, with the exception that Christ will have His headquarters in Independence, Missouri. At the end of this righteous period, a rebellious Satan will be crushed and the world will be transformed (Mayer, *RBA*, p. 455). The Mormons apparently believe in hell and that some non-Mormons will go there. However, there is very little explicit teaching on retribution. Smith's *Articles of Faith*, for example, have nothing on the future. Many think, as Mayer (*RBA*, p. 452), that "Mormons believe in universal salvation." Mormon doctrine concerning heaven is more detailed. There are three grades of heaven: telestial (lowest grade where unbelievers seem to go); terrestrial (for ignorant but honorable persons); celestial (for the good Mormons).

3 Terms Frequently Used by the Mormons

Aaronic Priesthood: One of the two priesthoods into which the Mormon hierarchy is divided, which includes the presiding bishopric, priests, teachers, and deacons.

Adam God: Doctrine that Adam was the Father God, based on the following statement of Brigham Young in the *Journal of Discourses:* "When the Virgin Mary conceived the child Jesus, the Father had begotten him in his own likeness. He was *not* begotten by the Holy Ghost. And who was the Father? He was the first of the human family. . . . Jesus, our elder brother, was begotten in the flesh by the same character that was in the garden of Eden, and who is our Father in Heaven" (I:50).

Apostles: The twelve men that are second in the Melchizedek Priesthood (subordinate only to the power of the presidency), who appoint the other officers and rule between presidential periods.

Baptism for the Dead: The practice of baptizing the dead by proxy, based on the Mormon interpretation of I Corinthians 15:29 that no dead person may go to heaven until baptized.

Blood Atonement: Apparently not officially recognized practice of shedding the blood of certain grievous sinners to atone for past sins and prevent still others in the future (cf. Brigham Young, *Journal of Discourses,* iv, 219; Stenhouse, *Rocky Mountain Saints,* p. 292 f.).

Book of Mormon: The record of extra-biblical, as well as much biblical history. The source of this information was allegedly golden plates, the location of which was revealed to Joseph Smith, who with the aid of the Urim and Thummim was able to translate them from the Reformed Egyptian hieroglyphics in which they were written.

Celestial Heaven: The highest heaven, reserved for faithful Mormons only.

Cumorah: Hill near Palmyra, New York. An impressive shrine today marks the spot where Joseph Smith is said to have found the golden plates from which he translated the *Book of Mormon.*

Deacons: The fourth order of the Aaronic priesthood, who assist the third level of officer, the teachers.

Doctrine and Covenants: Record of revelations subsequent to the *Book of Mormon.*

Elders: Sixth level of officer in the Melchizedek Priesthood. Elders preach, baptize, and perform other ministerial functions.

High Priests: The fourth level of the Melchizedek Priesthood, composed of the various presidents of the different stakes into which the community is divided.

Immortality: The Mormons teach a graded heavenly mortality which involves continued procreation.

Josephites: A minority of the followers of Joseph Smith claiming to be true to his principles (which are said not to have included polygamy) and his succession.

Lamanites: According to the *Book of Mormon* there were three migrations from the Bible lands. The last two (about 600 and 588 B.C.) combined in this country, forming the Nephites and the Lamanites. The Lamanites survived wars, living on as the American Indians.

Latter Days: Biblical prophecy of coming time of special outpouring of the Spirit.

The Manuscript Found: A romance by Solomon Spaulding, which most critics of Mormonism believe to contain the materials from which the *Book of Mormon* was actually constructed.

The Manuscript Story: The romance to which Mormon apologists usually refer when refuting the charge that the *Book of Mormon* was plagiarized from *The Manuscript Found.*

Melchizedek Priesthood: The first, and more important, of the two priesthoods, consisting of six offices: president, apostles, partriarch, high priests, seventies, and elders.

Moroni: An "angel," who revealed to Joseph Smith the location of the golden plates which recorded the story of the earlier history.

Nephites: According to the *Book of Mormon* there were three migrations from the Bible lands. The last two (about 660 and 588 B.C.) combined in this country forming the Nephite and Lamanites. The Nephites were later destroyed by war.

Patriarch: The nominal head of the Mormon hierarchy; an honorific title first given to the father of the Prophet.

Presiding Bishopric: The first division of the Aaronic Priesthood, charged with the collecting of tithes and the care of the wards.

Priests: These do a work similar to the elders but belong to the second order of priesthood, the Aaronic.

Revelation on Celestial Marriage: "Revelation on the Eternity of the Marriage Covenant, including Plurality of Wives, Given through Joseph, the Seer, in Nauvoo, Hancock County, Illinois, July 12th, 1843" served as the basis for the practice of polygamy. (Text in Stenhouse, *Rocky Mountain Saints,* pp. 176 ff.)

Seventies: These who go out as missionaries of the Mormon faith constitute the fifth division of the Melchizedek Priesthood.

Spiritual Wifery: A temple-performed marriage in which a spiritual affinity occurs between the partners and makes the marriage eternal.

Teachers: The third division of the Aaronic Priesthood that assists the priests and administers discipline.

Telestial Heaven: The lowest of the three Mormon grades of future existence where the wicked apparently dwell.

Terrestrial Heaven: An earthly paradise reserved for non-Mormons who are ignorant of the truth but are nonetheless honorable persons.

Urim and Thummim: The device which Joseph Smith used to translate the Reformed Egyptian hieroglyphics of the golden tablets into the *Book of Mormon.*

4 For Further Reading

Allen, Edward J. *The Second United Order Among Mormons.* 1936. Reprint. New York: AMS Press, n.d.

Anderson, Einar. *I Was a Mormon.* Grand Rapids: Zondervan, 1964.

Anderson, Rodger I. *The Bible and Mormonism.* Grand Rapids: Faith, Prayer, and Tract League, n.d.

Arbaugh, George B. *Gods, Sex, and Saints: The Mormon Story.* Rock Island: Augustana Press, 1957.

_____. *Revelation in Mormonism.* Chicago: University of Chicago Press, 1932.

Bennett, Wallace F. *Why I Am a Mormon.* New York: T. Nelson, 1958.

Berrett, William Edwin, ed. *Readings in L.D.S. Church History from Original Manuscripts.* Salt Lake City: Deseret Book Co., 1953.

Birrell, Verla L. *The Book of Mormon Guide Book.* Salt Lake City: Stevens and Wallis, Inc., 1948.

Brodie, Fawn M. *No Man Knows My History: The Life of Joseph Smith the Mormon Prophet.* Reprint. New York: A. A. Knopf, 1971.

Budvarson, Arthur. *The Book of Mormon: True or False?* (former title: *The Book of Mormon Examined*). Grand Rapids: Zondervan Publishing House, 1959.

Codman, J., *The Mormon Country.* 1874. Reprint. New York: AMS Press, 1972.

Cowan, Marvin W. *Mormon Claims Answered.* Salt Lake City: author, 1975.

Ericksen, Ephraim E. *The Psychological and Ethical Aspects of Mormon Group Life.* 1922. Reprint. Salt Lake City: University of Utah Press, 1974.

Fraser, Gordon H. *Is Mormonism Christian?* Chicago: Moody Press, 1957.

Gunnison, J. W. *The Mormons or Latterday Saints, in the Valley of the Great Salt Lake. . . .* 1853. Reprint. Plainview, N.Y.: Books for Libraries, n.d.

Hoekema, Anthony A. *Mormonism.* Grand Rapids: Wm. B. Eerdmans Publishing Co., 1963.

Hunter, Milton R. *Brigham Young, the Colonizer.* 1940. Reprint. Layton, Utah: Peregrine Smith, Inc., 1973.

_____. *Archaeology and the Book of Mormon.* Salt Lake City: Deseret Book Co., 1956.

Kirkham, Francis W. *A New Witness for Christ in America.* Independence: Zion's Press, 1951.

Lewis, Gordon. *The Bible, the Christian and Latter-day Saints.* Nutley, N.J.: Presbyterian and Reformed Publishing Co., 1966.

Linn, W. A. *The Story of the Mormons.* New York: Macmillan Publishing Co., 1923.

Martin, Walter R. *The Kingdom of the Cults.* Minneapolis: Bethany Fellowship, 1968.

_____. *The Maze of Mormonism.* Grand Rapids: Zondervan Publishing House, 1962.

Mulder, Wm. *Homeward to Zion: Mormon Migration from Scandinavia.* Minneapolis: University of Minnesota Press, 1957.

Mulder, Wm. and Mortensen, A. Russell, eds. *Among the Mormons: Historical Accounts by Contemporary Observers.* 1958. Reprint. Lincoln: University of Nebraska Press, 1973.

O'Dea, Thomas F. *The Mormons.* Chicago: University of Chicago Press, 1957.

Smith, Joseph. *The Book of Mormon.* Salt Lake City: Church of Jesus Christ of Latter-day Saints, n.d.

_____. *Doctrine and Covenants.* Salt Lake City: Church of Jesus Christ of Latter-day Saints, n.d.

_____. *The Pearl of Great Price.* Salt Lake City: Church of Jesus Christ of Latter-day Saints, n.d.

Smith, Joseph, Jr. *Inspired Version of the Holy Scriptures.* Independence: Reorganized Church of Jesus Christ of Latter Day Saints, n.d.

Smith, Joseph Fielding, comp. *Teachings of the Prophet Joseph Smith.* Salt Lake City: Deseret News Press, 1958.

Talmage, James E. *A Study of the Articles of Faith.* 36th ed. Salt Lake City: Church of Jesus Christ of Latter-day Saints, 1957.

_____. *The Vitality of Mormonism.* Boston: R. G. Badger, 1919.

Tanner, Jerald and Sandra. *Archaeology and the Book of Mormon.* Salt Lake City: Modern Microfilm Co., n.d.

_____. *The Case Against Mormonism.* 3 vols. Salt Lake City: Modern Microfilm Co., 1967-71.

_____. *Mormon Kingdom.* 2 vols. Salt Lake City: Modern Microfilm Co., 1969-71.

_____. *Mormonism—Shadow or Reality.* Salt Lake City: Modern Microfilm Co., 1972.

Turner, Wallace. *The Mormon Establishment.* Boston: Houghton Mifflin, 1966.

Wood, Wilford C. *Joseph Smith Begins His Work.* Salt Lake City: Deseret News Press, 1958.

5 Summary of Traditional Christian Doctrines

In the following chapter we present views which are held by the church without exception (unless so indicated). There are three main branches of the catholic (universal) church: Protestant, Eastern Orthodox, and Roman Catholic. These have differences among them, but there is a remarkable consensus of viewpoint on the basic structure of Christian doctrine. This fact is justification for use of the term "the catholic church." We have chosen quotations from official creeds of these branches to illustrate the various doctrines.

Doctrine of the Bible

The catholic church believes the sixty-six books of the Old Testament and New Testament to be the plenarily inspired Word of God. The Roman Church adds to this number some of the apocrypha. The Roman and Eastern Orthodox churches seem to give ecclesiastical tradition virtually equal authority with Scripture. The Protestant churches, however, hold to *sola scriptura*. Thus, the Lutheran Formula of Concord affirms: "We believe, confess, and teach that the only rule and norm, according to which all dogmas and all doctors ought to be esteemed and judged, is no other whatever than the prophetic and apostolic writings both of the Old and of the New Testament." The French Confession of Faith says of the Bible that "inasmuch as it is the rule of all truth, containing all that is necessary for the service of God and for our salvation, it is not lawful for men, nor even for angels, to add to it, to take away from it, or to change it." The American Revision of the Thirty-Nine Articles of the Church of England states: "Holy Scripture containeth all things necessary to salvation: so that whatsoever is not read therein, nor may be proved thereby, is not to be required of any man, that it should be believed as an article of the Faith, or be thought requisite *or* necessary to salvation."

Doctrine of God

The Athanasian Creed, accepted as an ecumenical creed by all branches of the church, reads: ". . . we worship one God in Trinity, and Trinity in Unity; Neither confounding the Persons, nor dividing the Substance [Essence]. For there is one Person of the Father, another of the Son, and another of the Holy Ghost. But the Godhead of the Father, of the Son, and of the Holy Ghost is all one, the Glory equal, the Majesty co-eternal. Such as the Father is, such is the Son, and such is the Holy Ghost. The Father uncreate, the Son uncreate, and the Holy Ghost uncreate. The Father incomprehensible [unlimited], the Son incomprehensible [unlimited], and the Holy Ghost incomprehensible [unlimited or infinite]. The Father eternal, the Son eternal, and the Holy Ghost eternal. And yet they are not three eternals, but one eternal. . . . So the Father is God, the Son is God, and the Holy Ghost is God. And yet they are not three Gods, but one God. . . . the Unity in Trinity and the Trinity in Unity is to be worshiped." The Westminster Shorter Catechism teaches: "There are three persons in the Godhead: the Father, the Son, and the Holy Ghost; and these three are one God, the same in substance, equal in power and glory."

Doctrine of Man

Again we may use the Westminster Shorter Catechism, for it expresses what all catholic churches believe about man. "God created man, male and female, after his own image, in knowledge, righteousness, and holiness, with dominion over the creatures."

Doctrine of Sin

The Roman Catholic statement made at the Council of Trent contains a catholic affirmation: ". . . Adam, when he had transgressed the commandment of God in Paradise, immediately lost the holiness and justice wherein he had been constituted; and . . . he incurred, through the offense of that prevarication, the wrath and indignation of God, and consequently death, with which God had previously threatened him, and, together with death, captivity under his power who thenceforth *had the empire of death, that is to say, the devil,* and that the entire Adam, through that offense of prevarication, was changed, in body and soul, for the worse. . . . this sin of Adam . . . [is] transfused into all by propagation, not by imitation. . . ." All catholic churches say at least this much; some, such as the Reformed, make more of the consequences of the Fall.

Doctrine of Christ

We may use the historic confession of the Council of Chalcedon (A.D. 451), for this has been recognized through the ages by all branches of orthodox Christendom as a true statement concerning the person of Jesus Christ. ". . . our Lord Jesus Christ, the same perfect in Godhead and also perfect in manhood; truly God and truly man, of a reasonable [rational] soul and body; consubstantial [coessential] with the Father according to the Godhead, and consubstantial with us according to the Manhood; in all things like unto us, without sin; begotten before all ages of the Father according to the Godhead, and in these latter days, for us and for our salvation, born of the Virgin Mary, the Mother of God, according to the Manhood; one and the same Christ, Son, Lord, Only-begotten, to be acknowledged in two natures, *inconfusedly, unchangeably, indivisibly, inseparably;* the distinction of natures being by no means taken away by the union, but rather the property of each nature being preserved, and concurring in one Person and one Subsistence, not parted or divided into two persons, but one and the same Son, and only begotten, God the Word, the Lord Jesus Christ. . . ."

We note that the expression, "Mary, the Mother of God," is a genuinely catholic expression. It does not mean that Mary was the genetrix of God, but that the human nature which was begotten in her womb was united with the eternal Son of God. So Mary was the mother of the child who was God; i.e., the mother of God.

Doctrine of Redemption

The satisfaction view of the atonement is the truly classic view of the catholic church. This could be shown from Protestant, Roman, or Eastern Orthodox creeds. We will show it by a citation from "The Longer Catechism" of the Eastern Orthodox Church: "Therefore as in Adam we had fallen under sin, the curse, and death, so we are delivered from sin, the curse, and death in Jesus Christ. His voluntary suffering and death on the cross for us, being of infinite value and merit, as the death of one sinless, God and man in one person, is both a perfect satisfaction to the justice of God, which had condemned us for sin to death, and a fund of infinite merit, which has obtained him the right, without prejudice to justice, to give us sinners pardon of our sins, and grace to have victory over sin and death."

There is a great difference among the three divisions of Christendom concerning the appropriation of this redemption achieved by Christ. The Protestant churches teach that it is by faith alone; the other branches incline to the view that it is by faith and works, or by faith considered as the beginning of works.

All branches of the church teach that the Christian has an obligation to endeavor to keep the moral law of God and that a person who does not do so is a reprobate. There is a doctrine in the Roman Church which is inconsistent with this, but nevertheless she teaches the above explicitly.

Doctrine of the Church

The Westminster Confession of Faith contains a definition of the church shared by all bodies of Christendom which accept the notion of the invisibility of the church. "The catholic or universal Church, which is invisible, consists of the whole number of the elect, that have been, are, or shall be gathered into one, under Christ the head thereof;

and is the spouse, the body, the fullness of Him that filleth all in all. The visible Church, which is also catholic or universal under the gospel (not confined to one nation, as before under the law), consists of all those, throughout the world, that profess the true religion, and of their children, and is the kingdom of the Lord Jesus Christ, the house and family of God, out of which there is no ordinary possibility of salvation."

Doctrine of the Future

While there has been less defining of the doctrine of the future by the catholic church than has been true of other doctrines, what has been stated is unanimously affirmed. All branches of Christendom are agreed that there is a place of eternal felicity, called heaven, where redeemed men and unfallen angels dwell in the gracious presence of God. It is also taught that there is a place of eternal misery, called hell, where all unredeemed men and fallen angels dwell in the wrathful presence of God. The Roman Catholic Church maintains, in addition, the existence of purgatory, the *limbus patrum,* and the *limbus infantum.* Universal salvation has been taught by various individuals, but no church recognized by catholic Christianity has affirmed it.

6 Brief Definitions of the Sects

Seventh-day Adventism teaches that salvation is attained by faith in the atonement made by Christ in 1844. This faith must be expressed in obedience to the ethical teachings of the Bible (including the law of the Saturday Sabbath) and in acceptance of the doctrinal teachings of the Bible (including the imminent premillennial return of Christ).

Jehovah's Witnesses claim to be the only consistent Bible students. They find the vindication of Jehovah to be the fundamental aim of history. This vindication is accomplished by the atonement of the first-born creature, Jesus, and expressed by the witnessing to an impending Armageddon. At this battle Jehovah and His Witnesses will be vindicated and the final consummation of things will begin.

Mormonism is built on a revelation subsequent to the Bible, called the *Book of Mormon*. According to this book, the church is to be reorganized on the basis of a creed which teaches a plurality of created gods, repudiates justification by faith, and teaches salvation achieved by the merit of obeying divine laws.

Christian Science is a formula for health and wealth by right thinking, but its thinking denies the reality of poverty and sickness.

CHART OF COMPARATIVE DOCTRINES

	Traditional Christian	Seventh-day Adventism	Jehovah's Witnesses	Mormonism	Christian Science
Bible	Verbally inspired	Reluctant to affirm verbal inspiration; vague about status of Mrs. White	Verbally inspired	Inspired Bible and Book of Mormon	Bible inspired and *Science and Health* is its inspired interpretation
God	Three Persons in one Essence	Approximately traditional Christian view	Uni-personal	Polytheism	Impersonal and pantheistic
Man	Body-soul created good	Body-soul creature, created neutral or with inclination to evil	Body. Soul not distinguishable from body	Pre-existent soul takes body at birth in this world	Soul only; body is an illusion
Sin	Result of Adam's Disobedience; corruption of nature and action	No clear doctrine of imputation of Adam's sin; man now polluted	Adam's sin brought liability to temporal death	It was necessary for Adam to sin. This brought mortality without guilt	"There is no sin" — it is illusion
Christ	One divine person in two distinct natures (divine-human)	Like traditional view but represents human nature as having tendency to sin	First-born creature; changed into man at birth in this world	Called creator but only pre-existent spirit who took body at incarnation	Christ is a divine idea; Jesus is mere human
Redemption	Faith in atonement as expressed by holy life	Believing in atonement made in heaven plus holy living including observance of Saturday Sabbath	Christ's ransom gives man chance to earn salvation	Atonement gives man chance to earn salvation	Salvation by casting out idea of sin
Church	Mystical union of all true believers, visable union of all professed believers	Seems to regard itself as true remnant church	Traditional church rejected 144,000 Witnesses make up church	Other churches apostate; efficient hierarchical organization	A denomination like Protestant, Roman Catholic, and Jewish
Future	Eternal heaven, eternal hell, temporary purgatory (R.C.)	Annihilation of wicked; millennium in heaven and eternity on new earth	Earthly millennium during which final probation leading to annihilation or eternal life	Pre-millennial reign at Independence, Mo.; tends toward universal salvation	Universal salvation in future when idea of sin gradually dies